Katherine HENGEL

Cool
LEAF LETTUCE

from
Garden to Table

How to Plant, Grow, and Prepare Lettuce

A Division of ABDO
ABDO
Publishing Company

visit us at www.abdopublishing.com

Published by ABDO Publishing Company, a division of ABDO, P.O. Box 398166, Minneapolis, Minnesota 55439. Copyright © 2012 by Abdo Consulting Group, Inc. International copyrights reserved in all countries. No part of this book may be reproduced in any form without written permission from the publisher. Checkerboard Library™ is a trademark and logo of ABDO Publishing Company.

Printed in the United States of America, North Mankato, Minnesota
102011
012012

 PRINTED ON RECYCLED PAPER

Design and Production: Anders Hanson, Mighty Media, Inc.
Series Editor: Liz Salzmann
Photo Credits: Aaron DeYoe, Shutterstock. Photos on page 5 courtesy of W. Atlee Burpee & Co.

The following manufacturers/names appearing in this book are trademarks: Inglehoffer®, Pompeii®, Hellmann's®, Marukan®, Roundy's®, Gedney®, Pyrex®, Kerr®

Library of Congress Cataloging-in-Publication Data
Hengel, Katherine.
 Cool leaf lettuce from garden to table : how to plant, grow, and prepare leaf lettuce / Katherine Hengel.
    p. cm. -- (Cool garden to table)
 Includes bibliographical references and index.
 ISBN 978-1-61783-185-0 (alk. paper)
 1. Lettuce--Juvenile literature. I. Title.
 SB351.L6H46 2012
 635'.52--dc23
                    2011037818

Safety First!
Some recipes call for activities or ingredients that require caution. If you see these symbols, ask an adult for help!

Sharp - *You need to use a sharp knife or cutting tool for this recipe.*

Hot - *This recipe requires handling hot objects. Always use oven mitts when holding hot pans.*

Nuts - *This recipe includes nuts. People with nut **allergies** should not eat it.*

CONTENTS

WHY GROW YOUR OWN FOOD?

Because then you get to eat it, of course! You might not be the biggest lettuce fan in the world. But have you ever had fresh lettuce? Straight from your very own garden? If not, prepare to be surprised. Fresh food tastes wonderful!

Plus, fresh food is really healthy. All produce is good for you. But produce that comes from your own garden is the very best. Most folks do not use chemicals in their home gardens. That makes home gardens better for you and the **environment**!

Growing your own food is rewarding. All it takes is time, patience, soil, water, and sunshine! This book will teach you how to grow leaf lettuce. Once it's ready, you can use it in some tasty recipes!

ALL ABOUT
LEAF LETTUCE

L ettuce has been around for centuries. We know that Egyptians have been eating it for more than 4,500 years! Today there are many **varieties** of lettuce. They all look, taste, and grow differently.

Leaf lettuce is one group of lettuce. It has loose leaves with curly edges. Its color can range from light green to red. Leaf lettuce tastes light and mild. But each variety tastes a little different from the others!

TYPES OF LEAF LETTUCE

ROYAL OAK LEAF

SALAD BOWL

BRAVEHEART

GREEN ICE

BUTTERCRUNCH

GROWING

In this book, you'll learn how to grow leaf lettuce in **containers**. Leaf lettuce is one of the easiest types of lettuce to grow. Plus, it grows fast. Let's get started!

When to Plant

Go online to find out the average date of the last frost in your area. **Sow** your lettuce seeds after this date.

The Right Conditions

Sunlight
Plants need sunlight to grow. Leave your lettuce plants in the sun for three to six hours a day.

Pests and Weeds
Be earth-friendly! Soap and water sprays keep pests away. White vinegar is a great weed killer.

Temperature
Once lettuce seeds **sprout***, the ideal temperature is 50 to 70* **degrees***. If it's hotter or cooler than that, bring the container inside.*

Shade
Plant in an area with some natural shade. Or use shade cloth to keep your plants cool when it is really hot out.

The Right Soil
Leaf lettuce needs a lot of **nutrients** *in its soil! Choose a loose* **loam** *that is rich in organic matter,* **nitrogen***, and* **fertilizers***.*

SEEDS

(1)

(2)

(3)

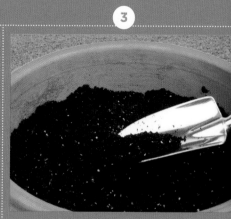

(1) Fill the **container** three-quarters full of soil. Wet the soil thoroughly.

(2) Sprinkle the seeds over the the soil. You'll thin the plants later, so don't worry about how the seeds are spaced.

(3) Lightly cover the seeds with ⅛ inch (.3 cm) of dirt. Water lightly.

4 Leaf lettuce seeds **germinate** in soil that is 45 to 70 **degrees**. If your climate is too warm or cold, start your seeds inside.

STAGES OF

Watering

Leaf lettuce loves water. Keep the soil moist, but not **waterlogged**. Before the **seedlings sprout**, use a spray bottle. After sprouts appear, use a watering can. Don't let the plants dry out!

Fertilizing

Lettuce likes to eat too! The more it eats, the faster it grows. The faster it grows, the better it tastes! For best results, add **fish emulsion** to your plants every week.

Thinning

Thinning means removing a few plants so others have room to grow. Leave 3 to 4 inches (8 to 10 cm) between plants. You can plant the ones you remove in another **container**.

WATER your lettuce plants whenever the soil is dry.

THIN the plants when the lettuce is about 2 inches (5 cm) tall.

FERTILIZE with fish emulsion every week.

MULCH right after thinning the lettuce.

GROWTH

Mulching

If you live in a dry climate, use **mulch** to keep the plants moist. After thinning the plants, spread a 2-inch (5 cm) layer of organic mulch around each one.

Trimming

Use a scissors to cut off the outside leaves. Try them in a salad! Removing the outside leaves helps the inside leaves grow.

Harvesting

You don't have to harvest leaf lettuce. You can just keep trimming it! But if you want to harvest it, use a scissors to cut the plants about 1 inch (3 cm) above the soil. That way they will grow back!

TRIM the lettuce when it gets about 3 inches (8 cm) tall.

HARVEST when the lettuce is 4 to 5 inches (10 to 13 cm) high.

9

HARVESTING

LEAF LETTUCE

1 Cut the plant with a scissors. Leave about 1 inch (3 cm) above the soil. It will grow back in a few weeks!

2 Separate the leaves. Fill the sink or a large **container** with cool water. Put the leaves in and swish them around. Then put them in a strainer and give the leaves one more rinse.

3 Spread some paper towels on the counter. Lay the lettuce on top and blot it dry with more paper towels. Use linen towels if you can.

4 Store the clean, dry lettuce in a plastic zipper bag. Push the air out before zipping it. Store it in the refrigerator. Lettuce will usually keep for six to eight days.

Leaf Lettuce

Q&A

How Come My Seeds Didn't Sprout?

You should see **sprouts** within one to two weeks. Be patient! Sometimes the seeds are planted too deep. Sometimes they get too much water. Just try again.

How Long Will it Take?

Leaf lettuce takes 40 to 60 days to **mature**. But growth has a lot to do with the sun and temperature. Leaf lettuce will grow the fastest in the summer.

Why Did My Plants Bolt on Me?

Leaf lettuce bolts, or turns to seed, near the end of its life. Bolting cannot be stopped once it's started. Leaf lettuce only lasts one season. You can look forward to planting more seeds next year!

DID YOU KNOW?

- *Lettuce is more than 90% water.*

- *The largest head of lettuce in the world weighed 25 pounds (11 kg)!*

- *Lettuce is the second most popular fresh vegetable in the United States!*

Cool Ingredients

AVOCADOS

BLACK BEANS

BLACK OLIVES

CARROTS

SHREDDED CHEDDAR CHEESE

CROUTONS

CRUMBLED BLUE CHEESE

CUCUMBER

CUMIN

DIJON MUSTARD

EGGS

GOLDEN RAISINS

HONEY

LEMON JUICE

LIME JUICE

LONG-GRAIN RICE

Some people are **allergic** to certain foods. This means they can get very sick if they eat them. They might need **emergency** medical help. Nut allergies are serious and can be especially harmful. Before you serve anything made with nuts or peanut oil, ask if anyone has a nut allergy.

MAYONNAISE

OLIVE OIL

ONION

PECANS

RAISINS

REFRIED BEANS

RICE VINEGAR

SALSA

SALT AND PEPPER

SOUR CREAM

SOY SAUCE

STRAWBERRIES

TOMATO

FLOUR TORTILLAS

VINEGAR

WHOLE-GRAIN BREAD

Kitchen Tools

BAKING SHEET

CAN OPENER

CUTTING BOARD

DINNER KNIFE

FORK

JAR WITH A LID

SHARP KNIFE

SERVING SPOON

MEASURING CUPS

MEASURING SPOONS

MIXING BOWLS

MIXING SPOON

SPIN THAT SALAD!

If you have a salad spinner you can skip the towels! Put the lettuce leaves in the spinner. Then give it a good spin. You'll see the water fly right off of the lettuce!

NON-STICK FRYING PAN

OVEN-SAFE GLASS BOWLS

SERVING BOWL

SPATULA

SPOON

STRAINER

TOASTER

PEELER

WHISK

Cooking Terms

Drizzle

Drizzle means to slowly pour a liquid over something.

Fluff

Fluff means to loosen or separate using a fork.

Roll

Roll means to wrap something around itself into a tube.

Peel

Peel means to remove the skin, often with a peeler.

Mash

Mash means to press down and smash food with a fork or potato masher.

Spread

Spread means to make a smooth layer with a spoon, knife, or spatula.

Toss

Toss means to turn ingredients over to coat them with seasonings.

Whisk

Whisk means to beat quickly by hand with a whisk or a fork.

SHREDDING LETTUCE

Some recipes call for shredded lettuce. To shred lettuce, put several clean leaves that are about the same size on top of each other. Roll them up. Then slice crosswise. Cut ¼ inch (.5 cm) off at a time. To cut something crosswise means to cut across its length. The pieces will be shorter, but the same width as the original.

SORT-OF
Sushi Rolls

Roll your own sushi with lettuce!

MAKES 4 ROLLS

INGREDIENTS

½ cup uncooked, long-grain rice

¼ cup rice vinegar

1 large, ripe avocado

1 carrot, peeled

1 cucumber, peeled

4 pieces of leaf lettuce, cleaned and dried

soy sauce

TOOLS

measuring cups

mixing bowls

mixing spoon

fork

peeler

cutting board

sharp knife

measuring spoons

1

① Prepare the rice according to the package instructions. Place the cooked rice in a medium-sized bowl, and spread it out. Pour the vinegar evenly over the rice. Pour it a little at a time. The rice should be slightly moistened. Gently stir with a large spoon. Let the rice mixture cool. Then fluff it with a fork.

② Peel the avocado. Remove the seed. Mash it until smooth.

③ Use the peeler to slice off thin strips of carrot. Cut the ends off of the cucumber. Slice it into ¼-inch (.5 cm) strips.

4 Spread about 1 tablespoon of mashed avocado onto a lettuce leaf. Add a few tablespoons of rice. Flatten out the rice. Place some cucumber and carrot on top.

⑤ Roll the lettuce leaf. Serve with soy sauce and rice.

2

3

5

ROCK-ON
Raisin Salad

Guaranteed to please all raisin lovers!

20

INGREDIENTS

2 tablespoons mayonnaise

2 teaspoons Dijon mustard

2 teaspoons honey

1 teaspoon lemon juice

pinch of salt

leaf lettuce, cleaned and dried

¼ cup raisins

¼ cup golden raisins

croutons

TOOLS

measuring spoons

jar with a lid

2 serving bowls

measuring cups

serving spoon

1. Make the dressing for the salad first. Put the mayonnaise, mustard, honey, lemon juice, and salt in the jar. Close the lid. Shake well.

2. Tear the lettuce into bite-size pieces. Put some in each serving bowl.

3. Put half of the raisins and golden raisins in each bowl. Use a serving spoon to drizzle dressing over the salads. Add croutons to taste.

To Taste?

Sometimes a recipe says to add an ingredient "to taste." That means you decide how much to add! Start small. You can always add more later. It's harder to remove something than it is to add more!

1

2

3

Breakfast Wrap

Chances are, you'll want these for lunch and dinner too!

MAKES 4 WRAPS

INGREDIENTS

2 tablespoons
refried beans

2 tablespoons salsa

3 eggs, beaten

1 tablespoon mayonnaise

4 flour tortillas

1½ cups shredded
lettuce *(see page 17)*

TOOLS

measuring spoons

mixing bowls

mixing spoon

non-stick frying pan

whisk

spatula

measuring cups

dinner knife

1 Put the beans and salsa in a small bowl. Mix until smooth. Heat the frying pan over medium heat.

2 Whisk the eggs in a small bowl. Pour the eggs into the frying pan. Wait about 1 minute. The bottom of the eggs should be slightly hard.

3 Pour the bean mixture over one half of the eggs. Use a spatula to flip the other half on top of the beans. Cook a couple more minutes until the eggs are set.

4 Spread some of the mayonnaise on each tortilla. Cut the eggs into four equal pieces. Put one piece on each tortilla. Cover the eggs with shredded lettuce. Roll up the tortillas.

1

2

3

4

BERRY GOOD
Vinaigrette Salad
Fresh berries make this tangy salad a sensation!

MAKES 2 SALADS

INGREDIENTS

2 tablespoons pecans, chopped

1 tablespoon vinegar

3 tablespoons olive oil

1 teaspoon lemon juice

salt and pepper

leaf lettuce, cleaned and dried

⅔ cup diced, fresh strawberries

2 tablespoons crumbled blue cheese

TOOLS

measuring spoons

cutting board

sharp knife

non-stick frying pan

mixing spoon

mixing bowls

whisk

① Put the pecans in the frying pan over medium heat. Stir them frequently until lightly toasted. Remove from heat.

② Make the dressing. Put the vinegar, olive oil, lemon juice, salt and pepper in a bowl. Whisk thoroughly.

③ Tear the lettuce into bite-size pieces. Put it in a large bowl. Add the toasted pecans, strawberries, and blue cheese. Toss with the dressing before serving.

1

2

3

THE AMAZING

ALT Sandwich

A tasty, tempting alternative to the BLT!

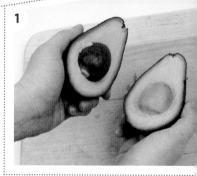

1

2

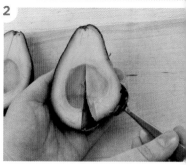

4

5

INGREDIENTS

1 avocado

4 slices whole-grain bread

2 tablespoons mayonnaise

8 large pieces of leaf lettuce, cleaned and dried

1 tomato, thinly sliced

TOOLS

cutting board

sharp knife

spoon

toaster

dinner knife

1. Cut all the way around the avocado lengthwise. Do not try to cut through the pit. Then twist and pull to separate into two halves.

2. Carefully remove the pit. Cut each half lengthwise. Do not cut through the skin. Use a spoon to gently scoop out the avocado.

3. Cut the scooped avocado into thin slices.

4. Toast the bread. Spread some mayonnaise on each slice.

5. Put two lettuce leaves on each slice of toast. Put tomato on two of the slices. Put avocado on the other two slices.

6. Turn the slices with tomato over on top of the slices with avocado. Cut each sandwich in half.

NACHO AVERAGE

Taco Bowl

Why dirty a dish when you can make your own?

MAKES 2 SALADS

INGREDIENTS

1 tablespoon lime juice

3 tablespoons sour cream

1½ tablespoons olive oil

1 teaspoon cumin

2 flour tortillas

olive oil

1 can black beans, rinsed

4 cups leaf lettuce, shredded (see page 17)

salt and pepper

1 cup cheddar cheese, shredded

1 small tomato, chopped

1 can black olives, drained

½ onion, finely chopped

TOOLS

measuring cups & spoons

mixing bowls

whisk

can opener

2 oven-safe glass bowls

baking sheet

strainer

sharp knife

cutting board

mixing spoon

1

(1) Preheat the oven to 400 **degrees**. Make the dressing. Put the lime juice, sour cream, olive oil, and cumin in a bowl. Whisk thoroughly.

2

(2) Microwave the tortillas for 10 seconds. Rub a thin coat of olive oil over each tortilla. Place two oven-safe glass bowls upside down on a baking sheet. Put a tortilla over each bowl. The tortillas should not touch the baking sheet. Gently press the tortillas around the bowls. Bake for 8 to 10 minutes.

4

3 Remove the tortillas from the oven. While they cool, warm up the black beans in the microwave. Put them in a bowl first.

(4) Put the lettuce, salt and pepper, and salad dressing in a large bowl. Toss well. Put half the lettuce mixture in each tortilla bowl.

5

(5) Put shredded cheese on each salad. Then add some warm black beans. Add the tomato, black olives, and onion last.

WRAP IT UP!

Did you enjoy growing food from the earth? Are you a gifted cook with fresh ingredients? Fresh ingredients go a long way toward making food taste great. Ask the best chefs in the world. They'll tell you! Fresh ingredients are their secret ingredients!

By now you know that fresh food tastes great. Plus, it's good for the **environment**. Food from your garden doesn't require **transportation** or packaging. It isn't covered in harmful chemicals either!

So keep at it. Don't lose that green thumb! Think about your favorite foods. Can you grow them yourself? Chances are, you can. Check out the other books in this series. There may be a book about growing and cooking your favorite food!

Glossary

ALLERGY – sickness caused by touching, breathing, or eating certain things.

CONTAINER – something that other things can be put into.

DEGREE – the unit used to measure temperature.

EMERGENCY – a sudden, unexpected, dangerous situation that requires immediate attention.

ENVIRONMENT – nature and everything in it, such as the land, sea, and air.

FERTILIZER – something used to make plants grow better in soil.

FISH EMULSION – a fertilizer made from liquid left over during fish oil production.

GERMINATE – to begin to grow from a seed.

LOAM – loose soil that has clay and sand in it.

MATURE – to finish growing or developing.

MULCH – something, such as straw or wood chips, spread over the ground to protect plants.

NITROGEN – a gas that is in all living things and makes up most of the earth's atmosphere.

NUTRIENT – something that helps living things grow. Vitamins, minerals, and proteins are nutrients.

SEEDLING – a young plant that grew from a seed.

SOW – to put seeds on or in soil so they will grow.

SPROUT – 1. to begin to grow. 2. a new plant growing from a seed.

TRANSPORTATION – the act of moving people and things.

VARIETY – different types of one thing.

WATERLOGGED – completely full of water.

Web Sites

*To learn more about growing and cooking food, visit ABDO Publishing Company on the World Wide Web at **www.abdopublishing.com**. Web sites about creative ways for kids to grow and cook food are featured on our Book Links page. These links are routinely monitored and updated to provide the most current information available.*

Index